My

First came Dad and Mom, then came the little baby.

Dad is a man,

Mom is a woman.

First, you're a little baby,

Then you grow into a big kid.

Use your tongue to taste yummy food—candy apples are so sweet!

Use your ears to hear sounds—the birds sing so beautifully.

Use your nose to smell—flowers smell so nice.

Use your eyes to see the world—cover them, and you can't see a thing!